She Believed She Could,
So She Did

■ WILLOW CREEK PRESS®

© 2020 Willow Creek Press

All Rights Reserved. No part of this book may be reproduced or transmitted in any form by any means, electronic or mechanical, including photocopying, recording, or by any information storage and retrieval system, without written permission from the publisher.

Published by Willow Creek Press, Inc.
P.O. Box 147, Minocqua, Wisconsin 54548

Printed in China

A STRONG WOMAN
LOOKS A CHALLENGE
IN THE EYE AND
GIVES IT A WINK.

WHEN THINGS
CHANGE INSIDE YOU,
THINGS CHANGE
AROUND YOU.

NEVER APOLOGIZE FOR BEING A POWERFUL WOMAN

IT TOOK ME A LONG TIME TO FIND MY VOICE AND NOW THAT I HAVE IT, I AM NO LONGER GOING TO BE SILENT.

A TIGER DOESN'T
LOSE SLEEP OVER
THE OPINION
OF SHEEP.

YOU'RE BRAVER THAN YOU BELIEVE & STRONGER THAN YOU SEEM & SMARTER THAN YOU THINK

HERE'S TO STRONG WOMEN.
MAY WE RAISE THEM.
MAY WE KNOW THEM.
MAY WE BE THEM.

IF PEOPLE ARE DOUBTING
HOW FAR YOU CAN GO,
GO SO FAR THAT YOU CAN'T
HEAR THEM ANYMORE.

DOUBT IS A KILLER.
YOU JUST HAVE TO
KNOW WHO YOU
ARE AND WHAT
YOU STAND FOR.

SHE IS CLOTHED WITH
STRENGTH AND DIGNITY;
SHE CAN LAUGH AT
THE DAYS TO COME.

I WILL NOT BE ANOTHER FLOWER, PICKED FOR MY BEAUTY AND LEFT TO DIE. I WILL BE WILD, DIFFICULT TO FIND, AND IMPOSSIBLE TO FORGET.

CHOOSE TO BE A FIRST-RATE VERSION OF YOURSELF INSTEAD OF A SECOND-RATE VERSION OF SOMEONE ELSE.

LOVE YOURSELF

Thank u, next

WOMEN ARE BLESSED
WITH ENOUGH PATIENCE
TO STAY AND ENOUGH
STRENGTH TO MOVE ON.

DON'T BE AFRAID.
BE FOCUSED.
BE DETERMINED.
BE HOPEFUL.
BE EMPOWERED.

BE YOU TIFUL

A STRONG WOMAN
STANDS UP FOR HERSELF.
A STRONGER WOMAN
STANDS UP FOR
EVERYONE ELSE.

SOME WOMEN FEAR THE
FIRE, SOME WOMEN
SIMPLY BECOME IT.

MEN, THEIR RIGHTS,
AND NOTHING MORE;
WOMEN, THEIR RIGHTS,
AND NOTHING LESS.

A GIRL SHOULD
BE TWO THINGS:
WHO AND WHAT
SHE WANTS.

I am no bird &
no net ensnares me.

IF YOU WANT TO FLY, GIVE
UP EVERYTHING THAT
WEIGHS YOU DOWN.

MAY YOUR CHOICES
REFLECT YOU HOPES,
NOT YOUR FEARS.

LOVE HER BUT
LEAVE HER WILD.

COURAGE IS THE BEST PROTECTION THAT ANY WOMAN CAN HAVE.

THE QUESTION ISN'T WHO'S GOING TO *Let Me* IT'S WHO IS GOING TO *Stop Me*

DOUBT KILLS MORE DREAMS
THAN FAILURE EVER WILL.

IF YOU GET TIRED,
LEARN TO REST,
NOT TO QUIT.

YOU ARE STRONG.
YOU ARE BEAUTIFUL.
YOU ARE ENOUGH.

"YOU'RE GOING TO BE HAPPY," SAID LIFE, "BUT FIRST I'LL MAKE YOU STRONG."

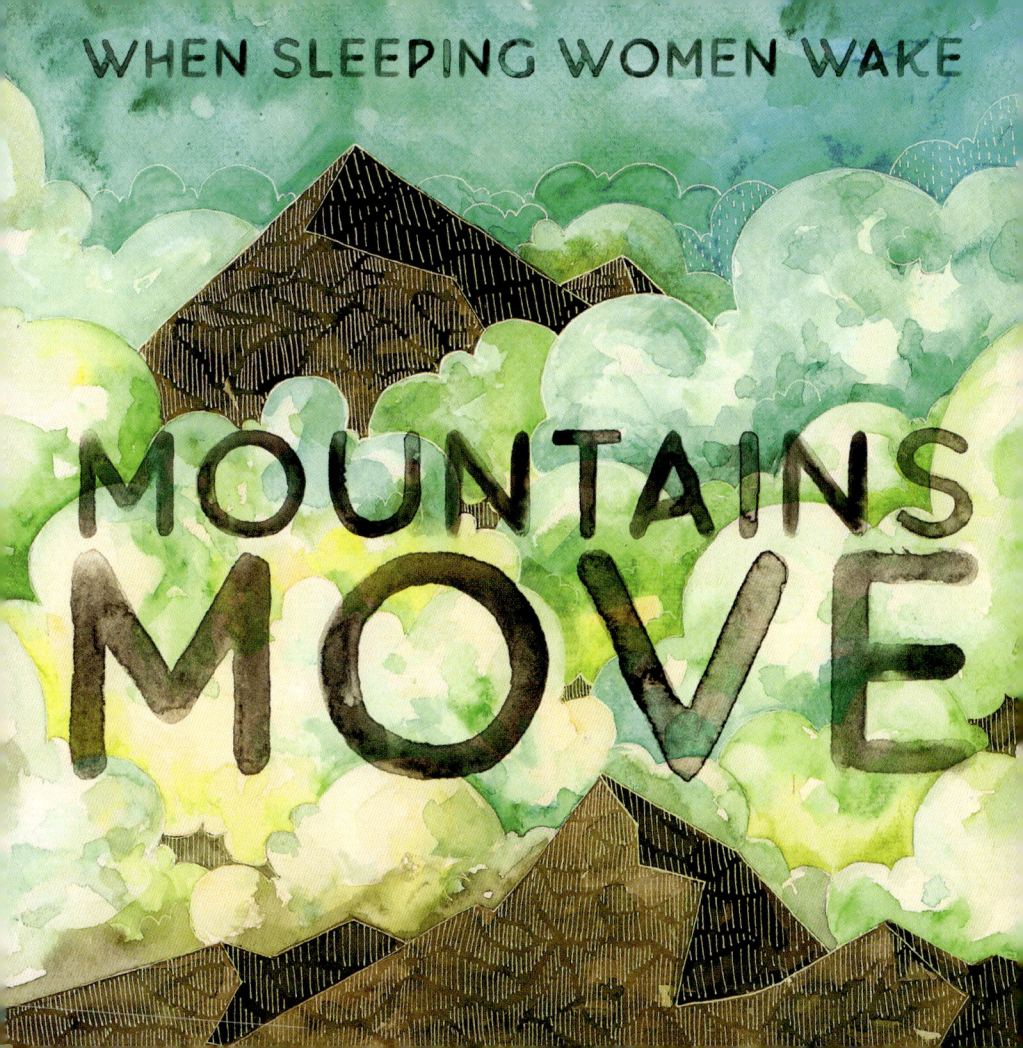

BE THE HERO OF
YOUR OWN BOOK.

THE MOST COURAGEOUS
ACT IS STILL TO THINK
FOR YOURSELF. ALOUD.

POWER'S NOT GIVEN TO YOU.
YOU HAVE TO TAKE IT.

THE SPACE IN WHICH WE LIVE SHOULD BE FOR THE PERSON WE ARE BECOMING NOW, NOT FOR THE PERSON WE WERE IN THE PAST.

Empowered women Empower women

I DON'T WANT OTHER PEOPLE TO DECIDE WHO I AM. I WANT TO DECIDE THAT FOR MYSELF.

ABOVE ALL, BE THE HEROINE OF YOUR LIFE, NOT THE VICTIM.

BE BOLD
BE BRAVE
BE YOU TIFUL

i am a woman what's your super power?

SOMETIMES THINGS FALL APART SO THAT BETTER THINGS CAN FALL TOGETHER.

THERE ARE 360 DEGREES, SO
WHY JUST STICK TO ONE?

THE MOST EFFECTIVE
WAY TO DO IT,
IS TO DO IT.

THE FUTURE BELONGS TO THOSE WHO BELIEVE IN THE BEAUTY OF THEIR DREAMS.

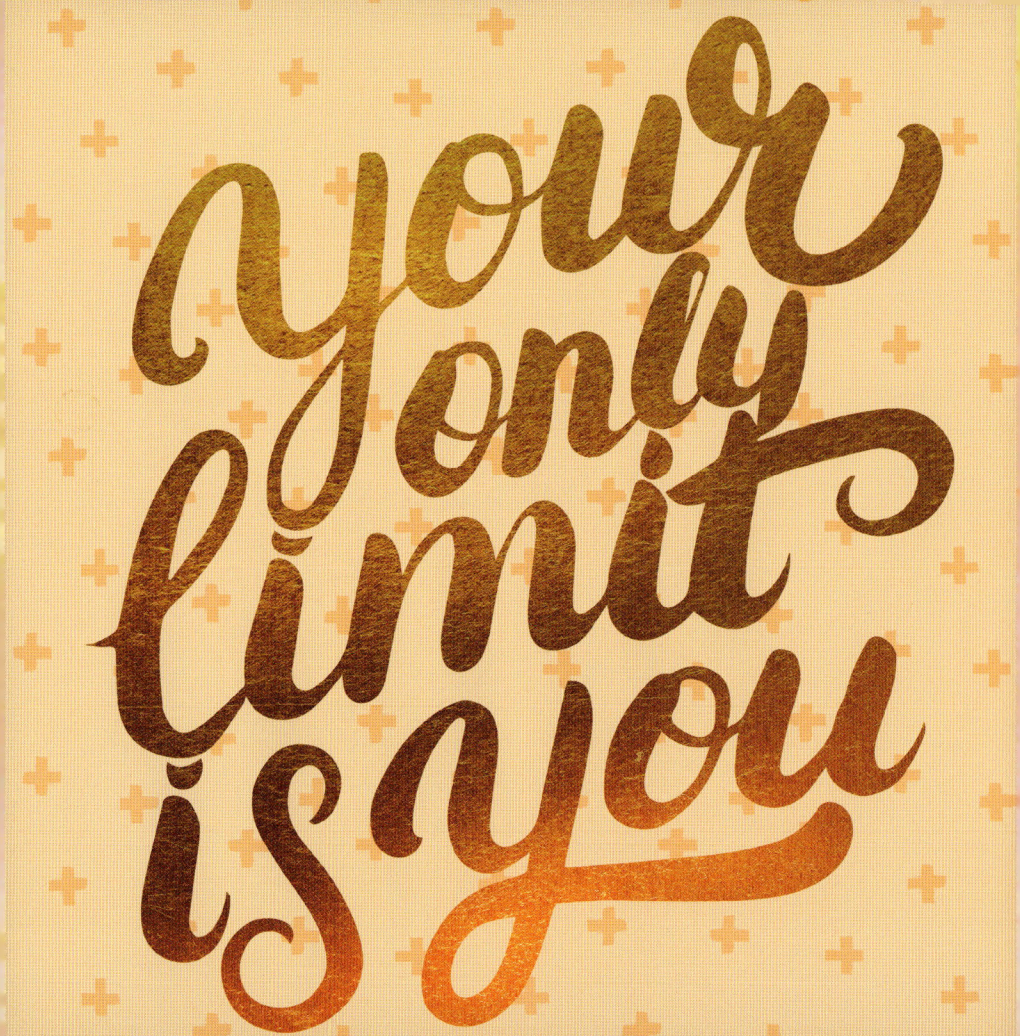

STRONG WOMEN DON'T HAVE ATTITUDES, WE HAVE STANDARDS.

I AM NOT A ONE IN A MILLION KIND OF GIRL. I AM A ONCE IN A LIFETIME KIND OF WOMAN.

~~*girl boss*~~
~~*boss babe*~~
~~*boss lady*~~
~~*mom boss*~~

JUST "BOSS" IS FINE

BE A VOICE,
NOT AN ECHO.

IF YOU STUMBLE MAKE IT
PART OF THE DANCE.

YOU'RE A DIAMOND DEAR, THEY CAN'T BREAK YOU.

GIVING UP DOESN'T ALWAYS MEAN YOU'RE WEAK. SOMETIMES YOU'RE JUST STRONG ENOUGH TO LET GO.

WOMEN ARE NEVER
STRONGER THAN WHEN
THEY ARM THEMSELVES
WITH THEIR WEAKNESSES.

IT ALWAYS SEEMS IMPOSSIBLE UNTIL IT'S DONE

A STRONG WOMAN LOVES,
FORGIVES, WALKS AWAY,
LETS GO, TRIES AGAIN,
AND PERSEVERES...
NO MATTER WHAT LIFE
THROWS AT HER.

ONCE YOU FIGURE OUT
WHAT RESPECT TASTES
LIKE, IT TASTES BETTER
THAN ATTENTION.

STAY STRONG.
MAKE THEM WONDER
HOW YOU'RE STILL SMILING.

IF THERE'S ONE THING
I'M WILLING TO BET ON,
IT'S MYSELF.

take a deep breath and begin.

IF YOU WANT SOMETHING SAID, ASK A MAN; IF YOU WANT SOMETHING DONE, ASK A WOMAN.